# COMEDY SCHOOL GUIDE TO STAND UP!

*Volume 1*

By: Lavell Crawford

ISBN: 978-1-7364329-0-7
Published By: InspiredByVanessa
www.InspiredByVanessa.com

# DEDICATION

This book is dedicated, first, to God and the Lord Jesus Christ, who's the head of my life. To my wife, Deshawn Jones, who holds me down all the time with love and support. To my mother, Anita Crawford, who would cringe and laugh even when I didn't get big laughs at home because I wanted to pursue this endeavor. And to all comedy clubs that gave me an opportunity to shine.

To Bruce Ayers and Che Che Stardom, Birmingham; Tom Sobel comedy caravan in Louisville; Al Canal in St. Louis; Funny Bone/Dave Carlow; Dave Stroupe; Funny Bone Columbus; Mike chuckles in Memphis; Joel Gray's stand-up live, Phoenix; Zaines in Nashville, Brian Dorfman and the late Dave Whiga (and his wife) of the Columbia House of Comedy.

To all the up and coming comedians and YouTube and social media personalities that have gained fame and are booming. Whether you're in the comedy club, or you are not ready, this book is for you. It is also for the novice and those who just want to understand why it's an art and how they can make a decent living from it.

I invite you to attend my Q&A seminar when I come to your

city. I hope it helps you to stay funny or get funny.

# INTRODUCTION

This is a guide book. It is not the holy grail to a successful stand-up comedy career. It's just my perspective. My name is Lavell Crawford, a 30-year veteran in comedy, and I have made a lucrative living in this wonderful world of stand-up, which launched me into other exciting areas of stand-up such as acting and public speaking and even winning acting awards. A short list of my attributes such as comedy half-hour specials on B.E.T., Comedy Central, HBO Def Jam, Shaquille O'Neal All Star (where I performed in series and even hosted one). I was the first runner-up on the long-running NBC comedy showcase, Last Comic Standing, and I shot a two-hour special titled "Can a brother get some love?" and "Home for the holidays," which aired on Showtime, Amazon Prime, and Netflix.

I was inspired to write this guide book because I get requests to watch upcoming comedians' sets, or I would get a lot of comedians seeking my advice on their stand-up or their journey into this fun adventure.

When I was coming into this stand-up world, it was as though there were gold rush comedy television shows, and comedy club chains were springing up every week. The great Johnnie Carson was making opportunities for stand-up. Arsenio Hall came on the scene with Dave Letterman and Conan O'Brien.

Comedians became the shot callers for a sitcom, sketch shows like SNL Mad TV and In Living Color, which opened doors for the urban comedy scene such as Def Jam, Comedy Jam, and B.E.T. ComicView, which is where I earned my first television appearance. Today, comedy is still prevalent as it ever was, but mainstream and urban comedy television venues have dried up, and this has given birth to the social media comics or internet comics getting booked by as many followers as they can get on each social media outlet. There's nothing wrong with that as long as you have goods to go with it because it's one thing to be funny in a 20-second recording, and it's another thing to hold a live audience captivated and laughing for 45 minutes. So, hopefully, I can help you get the tools needed to be a successful stand-up. I hope I can give a little 'insight.' It is said that as a true master, if you don't share something you know, it becomes a wasted gift.

# TABLE OF CONTENTS

# CHAPTER 1:

## DELIVERY

Everyone has their own setup and punchline back to back, with very high energy. A lot of this will get the crowd going pretty if it's a funny-enough material. It could have the audience in a frenzy. As long as you can keep that level of intensity going, the whole set will be fine. Good luck!

Hopefully, it's a short set that takes a lot of stamina and endurance, and every joke has to have that same punch.

For example:

Dave Chappell has a smooth mellow delivery, where his voice changes to bring his story to life.

Steven Wright can give a slow deadpan look and delivery that still produces big laughs.

Kevin Hart, Wanda Sykes, Bill Burr, etc., all have distinct voices that keep them in your face the entire while, so to speak.

But then you have some really innovative subliminal delivery where one joke has two punchlines such as that of Wendy Liebmann. But these are just examples, not guidelines, as everyone has their own style. I choose to use several styles to keep my audience on their toes, but all I've been sharing is that you should get on the stage and find your style of delivery. You could create your own song or flavor, and once you find your delivery, it will set you apart from every comic you share the stage with. So, get to finding the best approach to deliver your story.

# COMEDY SCHOOL GUIDE TO STAND UP!

_____

_____

_____

_____

_____

_____

_____

_____

_____

_____

_____

_____

_____

_____

_____

_____

_____

_____

_____

_____

_____

_____

_____

_____

_____

# LAVELL CRAWFORD

_____

_____

_____

_____

_____

_____

_____

_____

_____

_____

_____

_____

_____

_____

_____

_____

_____

_____

_____

_____

_____

_____

# LAVELL CRAWFORD

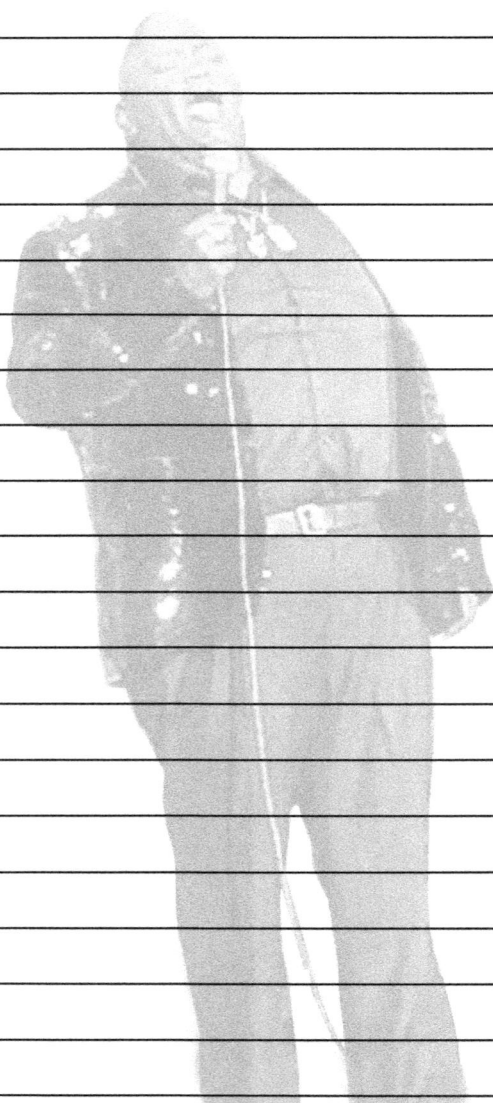

_____

_____

_____

_____

_____

_____

_____

_____

_____

_____

_____

_____

_____

_____

_____

_____

_____

_____

_____

_____

# COMEDY SCHOOL GUIDE TO STAND UP!

_____

_____

_____

_____

_____

_____

_____

_____

_____

_____

_____

_____

_____

_____

_____

_____

_____

_____

_____

_____

_____

_____

# CHAPTER 2:

# TIMING

This word 'timing' is an adjective of the word 'time,' which means finding the right moment to attack or strike to gain a result or outcome you were attempting to achieve from a battle in a war or a fight. For those who watch sports or play chess, if you are focused, you will find the right timing that comes with stage time, and that's how you have to treat stand-up. And like a chess match, getting your jokes and making them funny all ties into timing. Listed below are elements of timing:

- Shock value: How to get the attention of the masses. A lot of that works with timing. Talking about the obvious, from physical appearance to something the audience doesn't expect coming from you—e.g., yelling or something off-color.

- The rhythm of the laughter: Once you start getting on stage, you will start feeling this rhythm. It will start revealing itself the more you gain experience. You will start hearing the burst and fluctuations, and then when it slows down, you throw another jab with the same energy.

- Timing will dictate how funny a joke or strong of an impact a punchline will be to your audience. An attentive, quiet audience can be a great audience.

  It is said that silence is golden but only if you can turn that silence into a burst of laughter. I prefer gaining the attention of a little talkative crowd or audience than a quiet, attentive group that isn't reacting or laughing. This can be a little devastating, but hard work and stage time will help you have less and less, hopefully. LOL!

- Timing, to me, is like jumping a rope, switching lanes on a fast highway, or throwing the knockout punch in a fight. Finding your moments on stage is something that can't be written; it has to be experienced. That comedy muscle will get stronger; it will become second nature.

# LAVELL CRAWFORD

_____

_____

_____

_____

_____

_____

_____

_____

_____

_____

_____

_____

_____

_____

_____

_____

_____

_____

_____

_____

_____

_____

_____

_____

_____

_____

_____

_____

_____

_____

_____

_____

_____

_____

_____

_____

_____

_____

_____

_____

_____

_____

_____

# LAVELL CRAWFORD

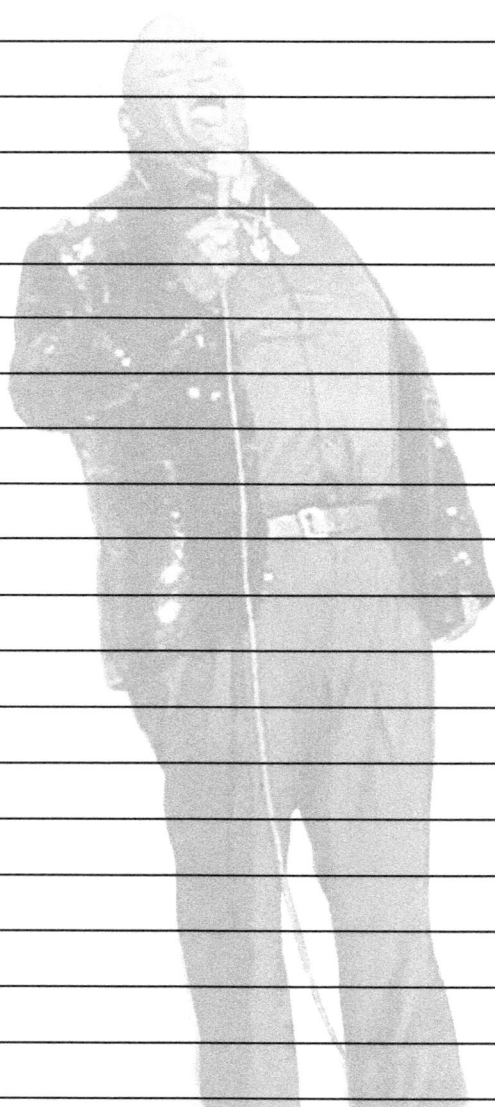

# COMEDY SCHOOL GUIDE TO STAND UP!

_____

_____

_____

_____

_____

_____

_____

_____

_____

_____

_____

_____

_____

_____

_____

_____

_____

_____

_____

_____

_____

_____

_____

_____

_____

# LAVELL CRAWFORD

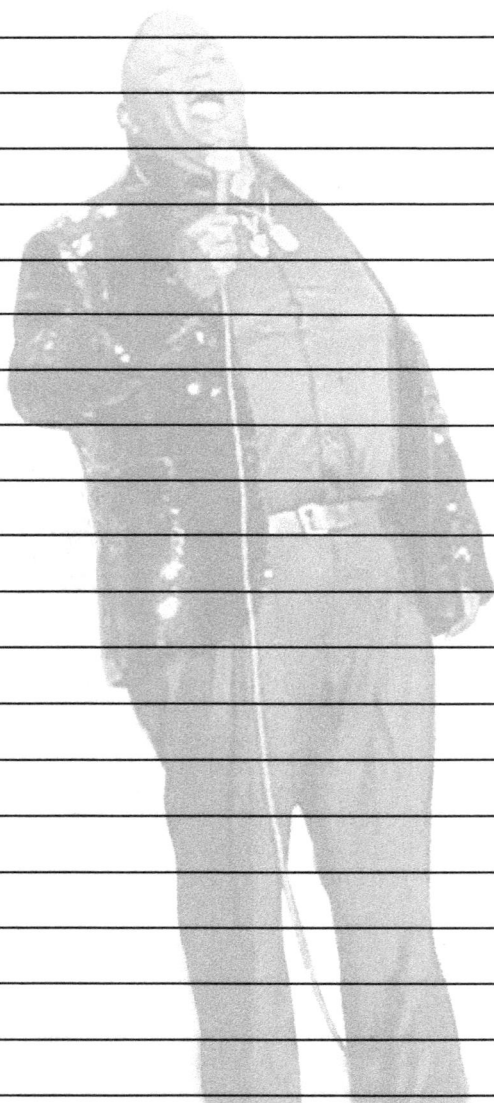

# CHAPTER 3:

# STAGE PRESENCE

Controlling your audience has a unique way of gaining their attention and bringing your jokes back to life. Here are a few ways to do this:

- Always face your audience, even if you have to focus on one person or something that can help you stay in your moment. 'Pro Tips' finds that one very attentive audience member who is giving you that positive feedback or laughter can help you stay in your story.

- Creating a fourth wall: This is an actor's terminology specifically for stage plays because, the majority of the time, like a comedian, they are performing in front of a live audience, and what this means is that you want to stay in character. No matter how the audience reacts, you always keep a game face on.

- Command the stage: You have the opportunity from the first five to fifteen minutes to command the stage. You can do a open mic set or a hosting set You ought to have some ideas as to how to command a stage, and the best way to achieve this is to act like you know what you are doing. Never let the audience see you sweat unless you are a big guy only then can you sweat all you like, and the more you do this, the more you build your confidence into a commanding performance.

And that's where POV comes in, which is your point of view. And just like it sounds, it depends on how you see certain subjects like I mentioned earlier in this guide. Everyone sees a car crash or a fight, and every person views it differently, and your way of describing it is how you always deliver your jokes.

Basically, find your character. Your character evolves as you do the work, and it will change as you grow more comfortable on stage. And that helps you find your voice, which is your stand on something. A lot of times, what you hear a comic say on stage are his/her true thoughts and feelings. They may have attempted or done them, no matter how strange or ridiculous it may sound, but that's what makes comedy so great because you can be crazy, and everybody laughs at your psychosis as long as it is funny enough.

So, become fearless with your craft. Every time you see an open mic or a bar with a mic or talent showcase, always believe that you're the funniest son of b%^ch in the building and the world.

Well, like I said, this comedy guide is not guaranteed to make you a stand-up comic or even a successful comic, but it will give you some insight into how to get started, and the rest is up to you to be fucking funny. And if you don't get funny, don't blame my guide; you just didn't read it right. Love.

# LAVELL CRAWFORD

# COMEDY SCHOOL GUIDE TO STAND UP!

_____

_____

_____

_____

_____

_____

_____

_____

_____

_____

_____

_____

_____

_____

_____

_____

_____

_____

_____

_____

_____

_____

# LAVELL CRAWFORD

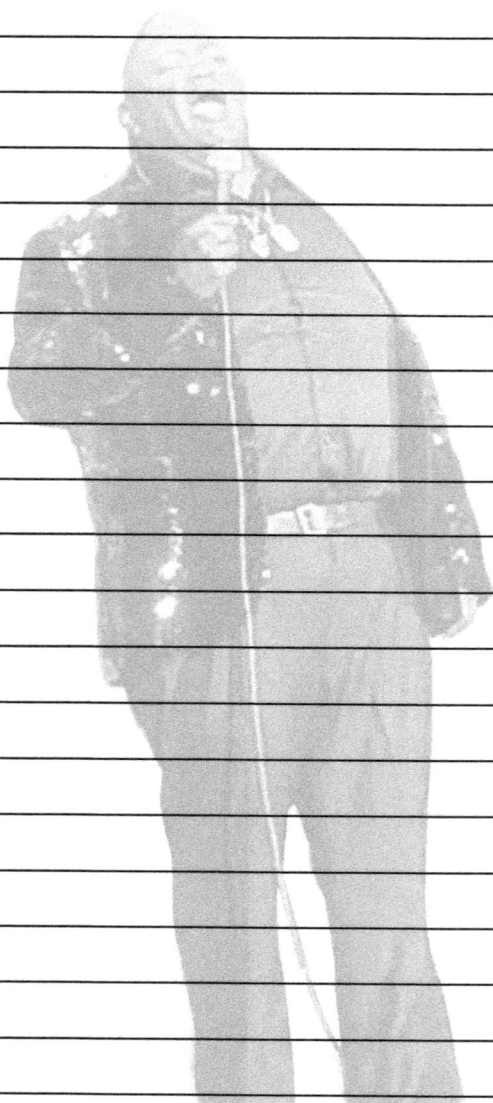

# LAVELL CRAWFORD

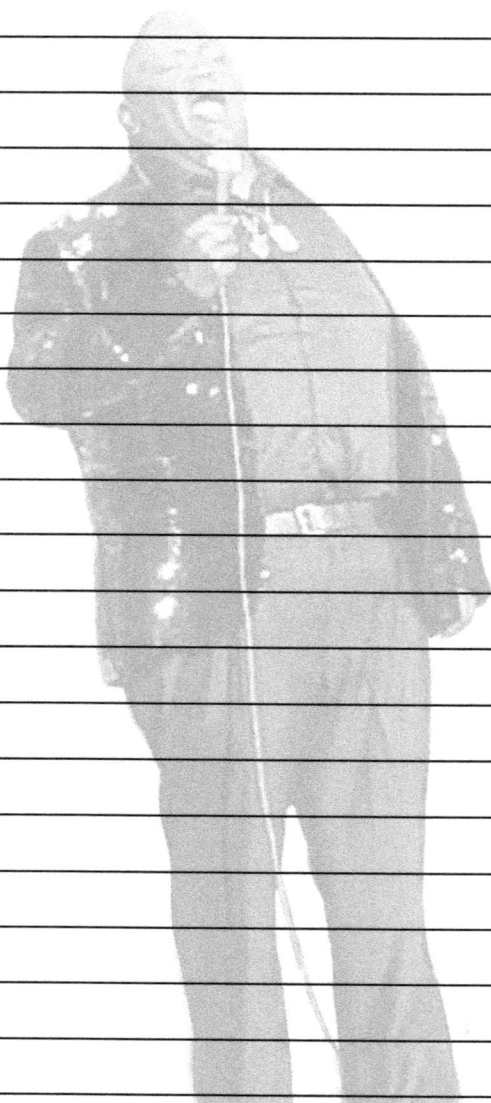

_____

_____

_____

_____

_____

_____

_____

_____

_____

_____

_____

_____

_____

_____

_____

_____

_____

_____

_____

_____

_____

_____

_____

_____

# CHAPTER 4:

# REASONS TO DO AND NOT DO STAND-UP COMEDY

What made me catch the comedy bug was: being in college, not knowing what I was going to do, and failing a lot. I lost my grants. I was a member of the Black Student Union program, and we were able to book some entertainment. They had a few mainstreams (white comics) who were funny, but the black students weren't attending the shows, though I went because it intrigued me. So, the Black Student Union was able to book an urban act, which happened to be a comedy legend on the rise Mr. Sinbad. He was great, and that fueled my fire even more because the only black comedian I knew before seeing him was the legendary Richard Pryor. I always listened to his comedy albums, so this opened up a whole new world to me. I knew then that this was what I wanted to do because I used to make my friends and family laugh, but nobody ever encouraged me to venture into pursuing my passion, and if they did, they were hoping I fall on my face and never try it again but nope; I didn't. 'Doubt' was always my fuel for success. When somebody didn't believe in me, it made me strive harder to prove them wrong, and I did. Oh yes, I did.

Reasons to do stand-up comedy:

- You have to have respect for the art because you are painting a well-illustrated picture in a stranger's mind a stranger who doesn't know and may never have had the experience that you are talking about, but through you, they are living it.

- You can feel the energy or the force inside you saying, "I've got to, at least, try it once."

- Have no expectations: You are excited about the unexpected; you are not trying to blow up doing stand-up. Instead, welcome all the perks that come from it such as a pat on the back, a thumbs-up, or something major like stardom.

- You've got a story to tell: A story is always funnier than a joke to me because people remember a story, and it lets the audience go on this wild ride with you. A lot of comedians tell the same or similar jokes, but they never tell your story, and if they do, they never tell it like you do because they have not lived your story, even if it's relatable.

- You never want to have someone else try to tell you to get on stage. You must have the passion in you so it satisfies someone else's passion for your gift. Otherwise, you have squandered your gift from God.

The adventure of stand-up is so fun and fulling you will never experience another moment like it in your life.

This great power is learned and has to be harnessed and controlled to stand on stage flat-footed, telling your story to strangers who have no reason to even listen to you. But once you learn to embrace this great ability to have the audience pondering and anticipating your every word, every facial expression, the hilarious quips and ideas that spew from your joke factory (which is your brain), you become enchanted and intoxicated in your power. But a great quote from Spiderman's uncle Ben Parker goes thus: "With great power comes great responsibility." So, when you have the audience eating out of the palm of your hand, you have to remember they deserve your best.

## Reason not to do it:

- Honestly, there is no reason not to do comedy because I fell in love with it once I hit that stage, and it never gets old.
- One reason not to do comedy is if you think it's going to be an overnight success. Don't bullshit yourself. Ask Eddie Murphy, Chris Rock, or Dave Chappell it never happened overnight. They all woke the next day to try it again.
- If you are doing comedy because everyone else thinks you're funny, there's nothing wrong with moral support, but if it's not your passion, STOP! You are in the way!

- If you think you're funnier than most people making it today, apparently you are an asshole, and I'd love for you to get your ass on the stage and get your ass handed to you. Here's one thing you must know: every comedian or comedienne went through a trial by fire to attain their current success.
- If you can't take rejection, stay away from the stage.
- But if you want to do something that will teach you to develop a talent that you will hone, something that will give you instant gratification and make you feel you had a superpower, then welcome to stand-up. And always remember: anyone can tell a joke, but everyone can't do stand-up.

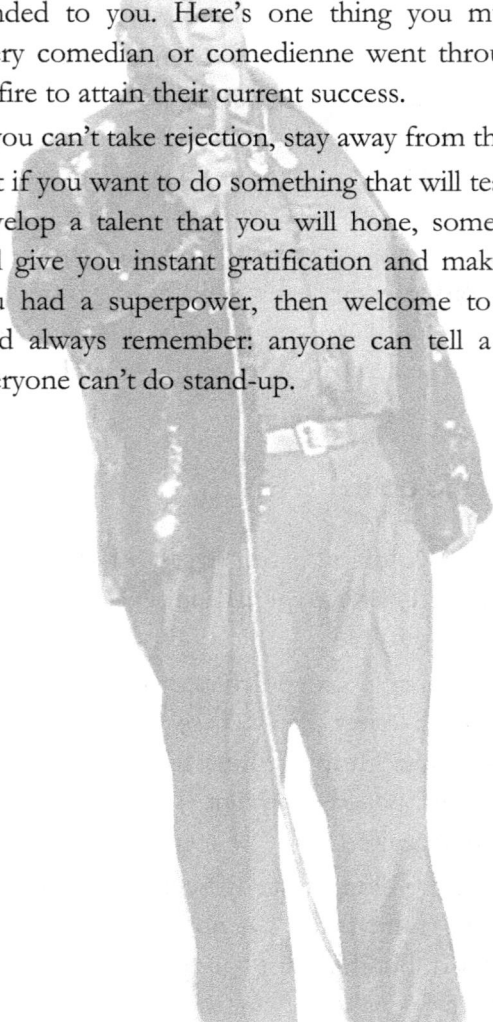

# LAVELL CRAWFORD

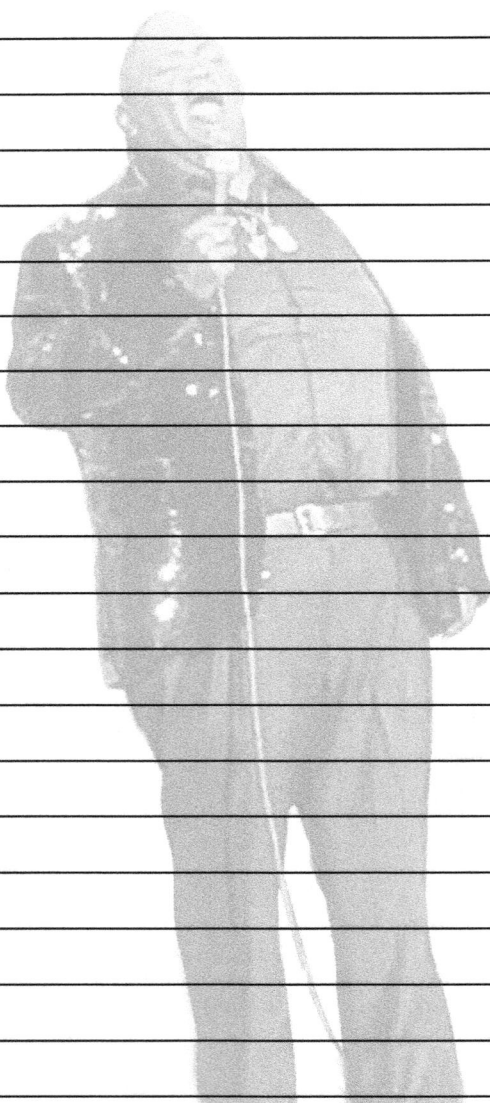

_____

_____

_____

_____

_____

_____

_____

_____

_____

_____

_____

_____

_____

_____

_____

_____

_____

_____

_____

_____

_____

_____

_____

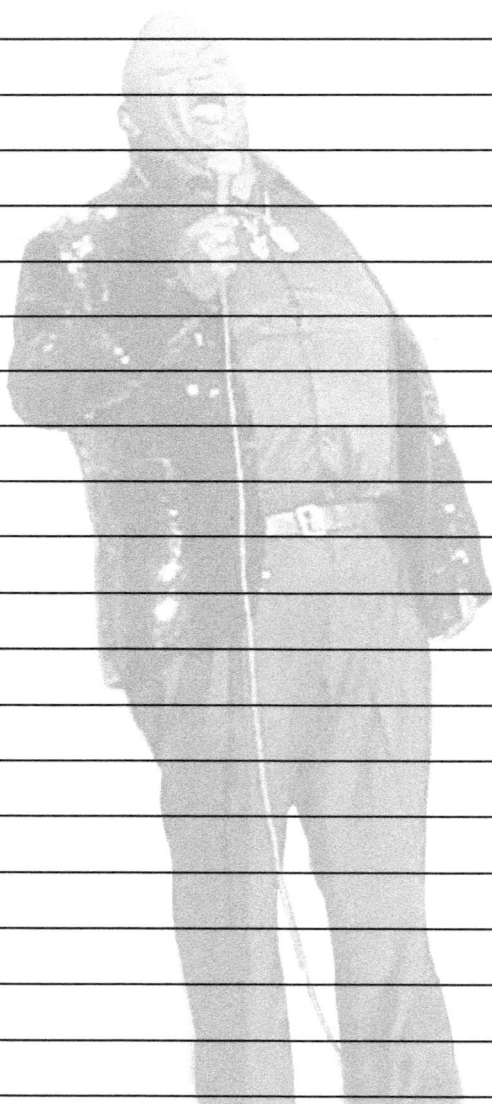

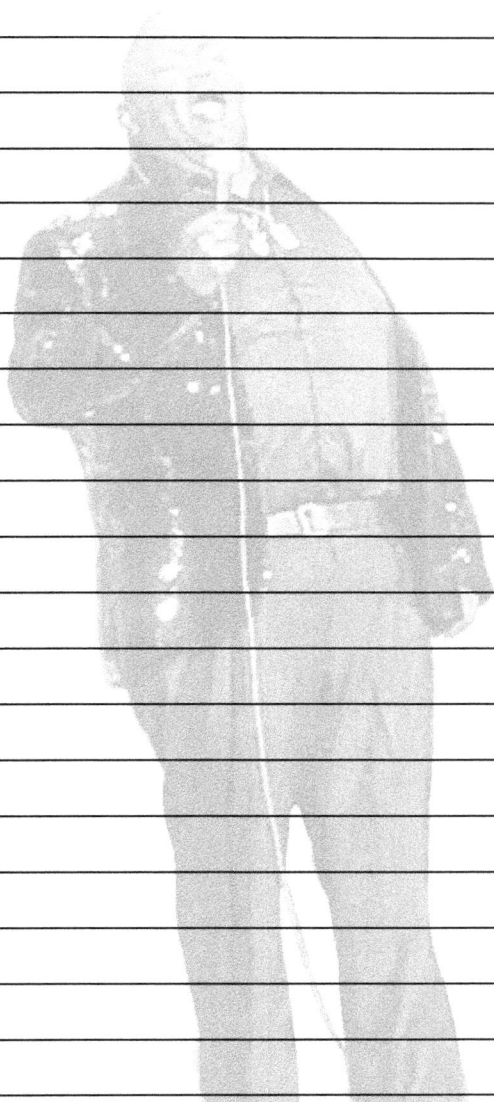

_____

_____

_____

_____

_____

_____

_____

_____

_____

_____

_____

_____

_____

_____

_____

_____

_____

_____

_____

_____

_____

_____

_____

# CHAPTER 5:

# MATERIAL

The reason why it's call material is that what you will use to build your set should comprise a few factors:

1. Something relative: You should never try to please the audience; that's not your job. Your job is to make them laugh, and one of the best ways to do that is by talking about something that could make some audience members say "Hey, that happened to me," but your own version helps set the tone and radiates comfortable energy.

2. Nothing is off-limits, but be aware that you may lose some of your audience. However, confidence will keep their attention. So, don't be afraid to write fearlessly.

3. Material is mainly written on stage. It's like being a scientist because trying new jokes on an audience is your experiment. So, see what joke works or doesn't. Your subject can be about anything you find humor in.

4. Jokes consist of four vital parts:
   - Setup
   - Story
   - Punchline
   - Point of view
5. Make it all funny from the way you see the world. What this means is, you find a way of drawing or capturing your audience's attention. There is no one way of achieving this methodology. You have to find your attention-getter from voice inflection. It could either be dazzling comical or outlandish, but the main thing about the setup is gaining the attention of the crowd so they can hear your story. One personal tip I can give is, I always use a metaphor that I'm the finest lady in the room/comedy club, so all eyes on me because I am sexy!

Story: This means bringing oneself on the stage, basically personalizing your set because, just like a song, no one should be able to tell your story like you can no matter how real, funny, dark, or exaggerated your story is. Please, work on making it interesting. Do your best to keep your audience riveted. These days, people go about with smartphones, and their short attention span and social media distraction may be a challenge.

So, the best way to achieve this skill is to practice and experiment with several different techniques. Watch veterans. Don't copy them; just see what makes them a veteran, and always remember every time you hit the stage, the energy will be different sometimes high sometimes low and sometimes really chaotic but perseverance births success, and success helps you fall in love with the career even more.

Punchlines: The word 'punch' means forceful impact toward an opposition, which in this case is the meat of the joke or story you are sharing with your audience. I like to put many smaller punchlines in the joke leading up to the big punchline at the end of the joke or story, and you want it to be highly climatic, so you have to draw or bait your audience. You have to find a way to put a scene on their (your audience) mind. The best way to do this is to make clear what you're talking about. Describe it so well they feel they were there with you. Your punchline is the ride you took them on.

Point of view: This is basically your voice, the way you see the funny in anything, and how you make it funny to your audience. Like I have said before, two people could see an incident and tell totally different stories. Your point of view is the way you bring your story into your world.

# LAVELL CRAWFORD

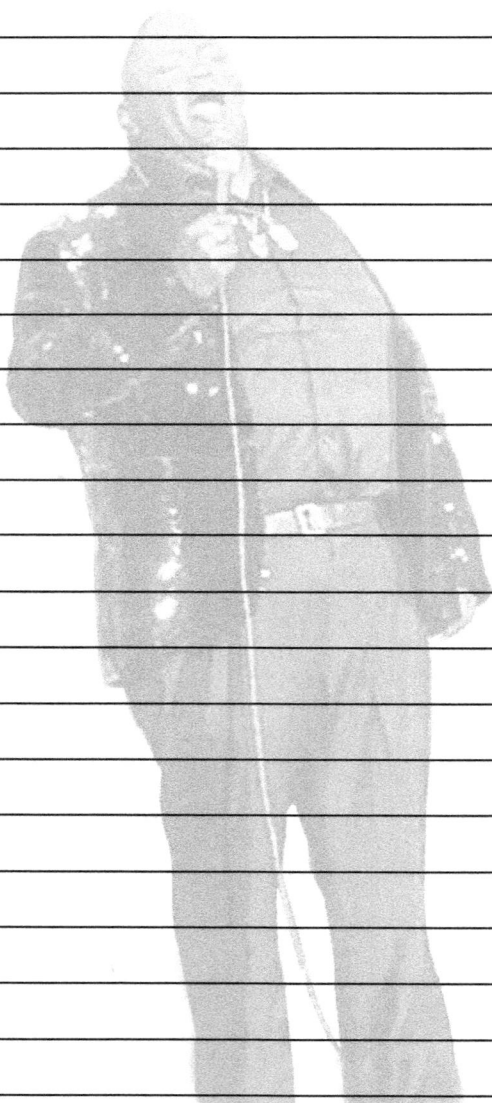

# LAVELL CRAWFORD

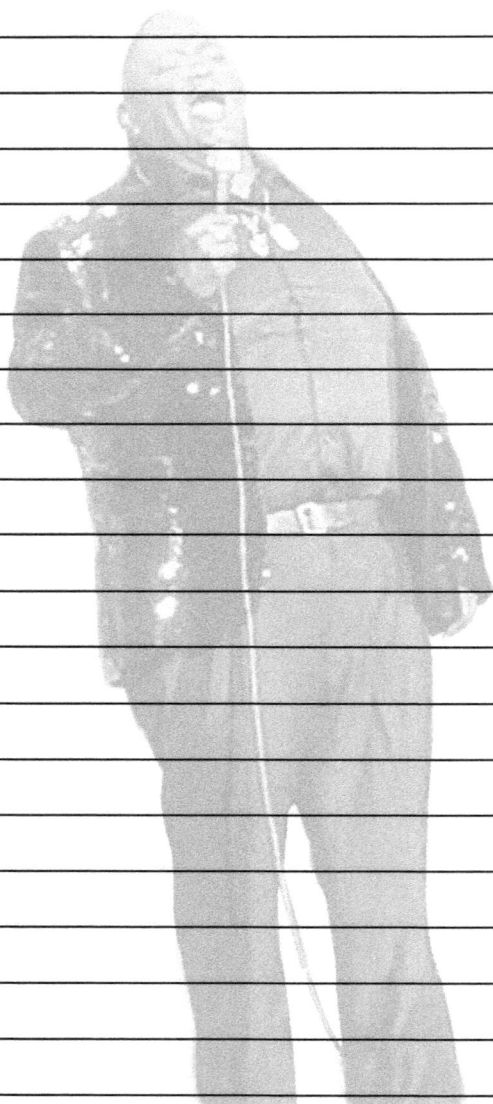

# COMEDY SCHOOL GUIDE TO STAND UP!

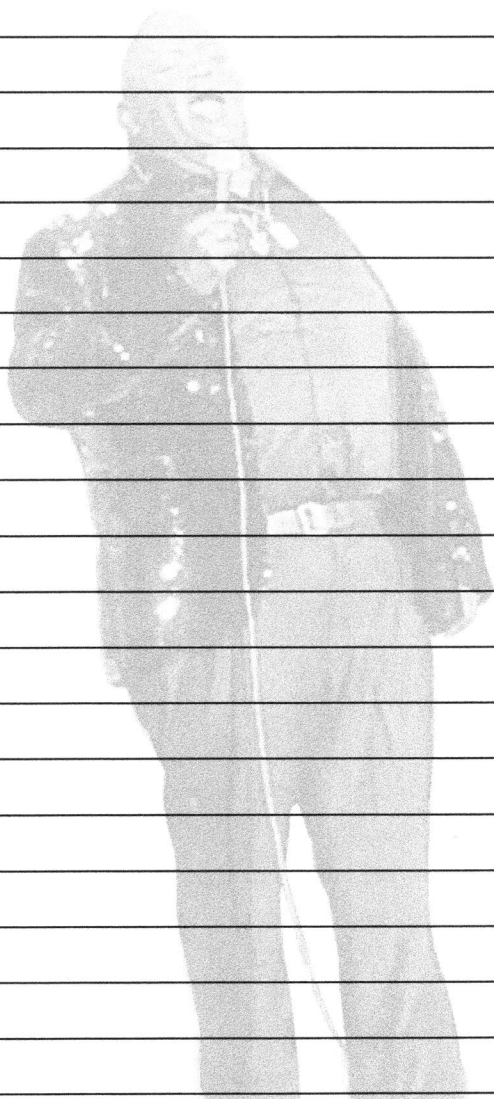

_____

_____

_____

_____

_____

_____

_____

_____

_____

_____

_____

_____

_____

_____

_____

_____

_____

_____

_____

_____

_____

_____

# CHAPTER 6:

# HOW TO GET STAGE TIME

These little droplets of ideas are just methods that I have explored or even witnessed, but there are many ways of getting stage time. None is better than the other. Stage time is like working out in the gym to get your comedic muscles strong, and the muscles are your timing, delivery style, and most importantly the material. So, find yourself some stage by any means necessary:

- Google local comedy clubs and see what day is their open mic night. Go in person and see how to get on the list.
- Hang with other comics. They always know where the spots are and who to talk to.
- Be accessible to the comedy club: A lot of comedians and comediennes do odd jobs, ranging from working at the club to being an Uber with the headliner 'Comic pick-up from the airport if needed.' You can pass out flyers, etc. Anything you can do! Build relationships with nationally touring comics. You

never know; opportunities could come from it in the future.

- Stage time comes in many forms, such as talent shows, comedy contests, outdoor functions, bars, places that have live music, family reunions, etc. Stage time gives you the opportunity to get stronger and confident on stage.

- Build your own comedy night with lots of comics. Get adventurous. Every venue is looking for free advertising and entertainment. I've seen comedy night even in a laundromat.

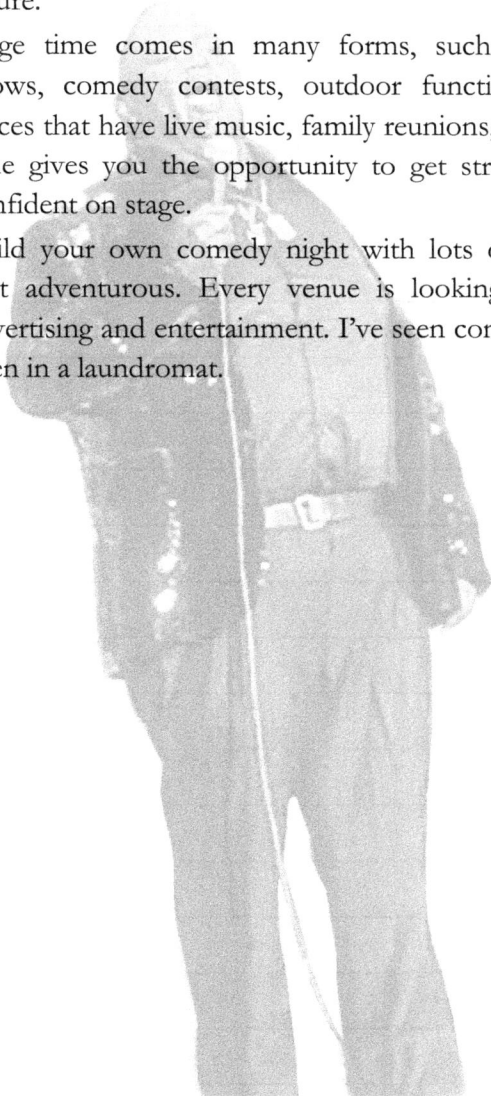

# LAVELL CRAWFORD

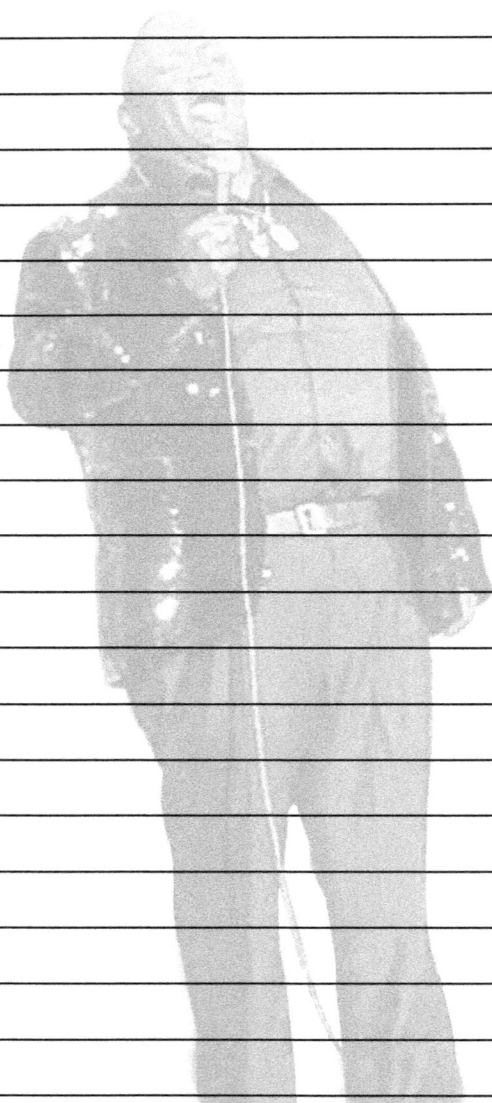

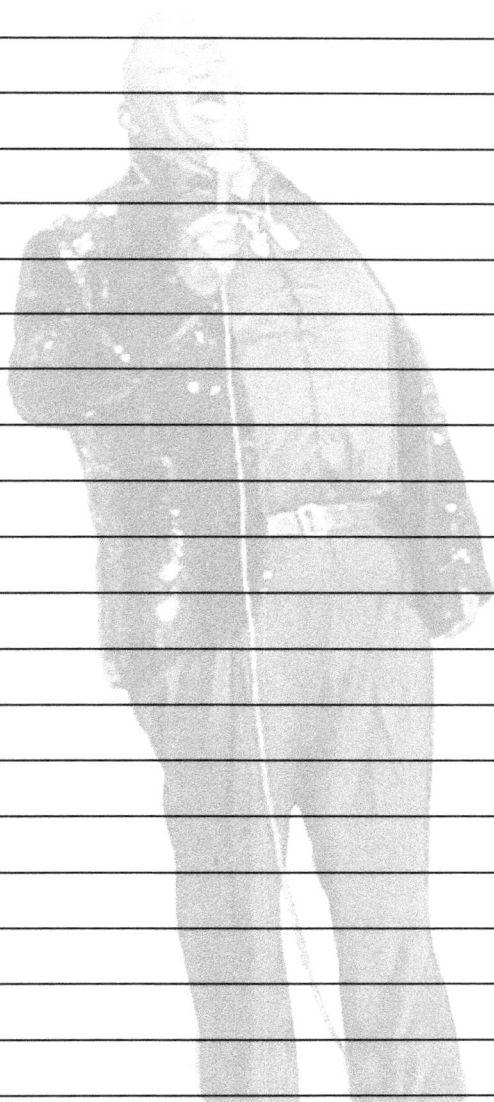

# LAVELL CRAWFORD

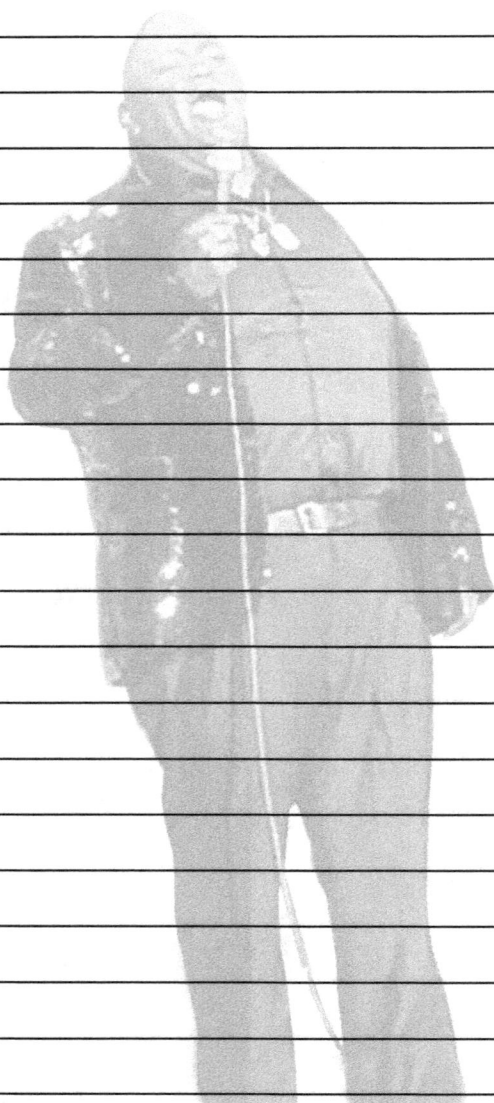

_____

_____

_____

_____

_____

_____

_____

_____

_____

_____

_____

_____

_____

_____

_____

_____

_____

_____

_____

_____

_____

_____

_____

# LAVELL CRAWFORD

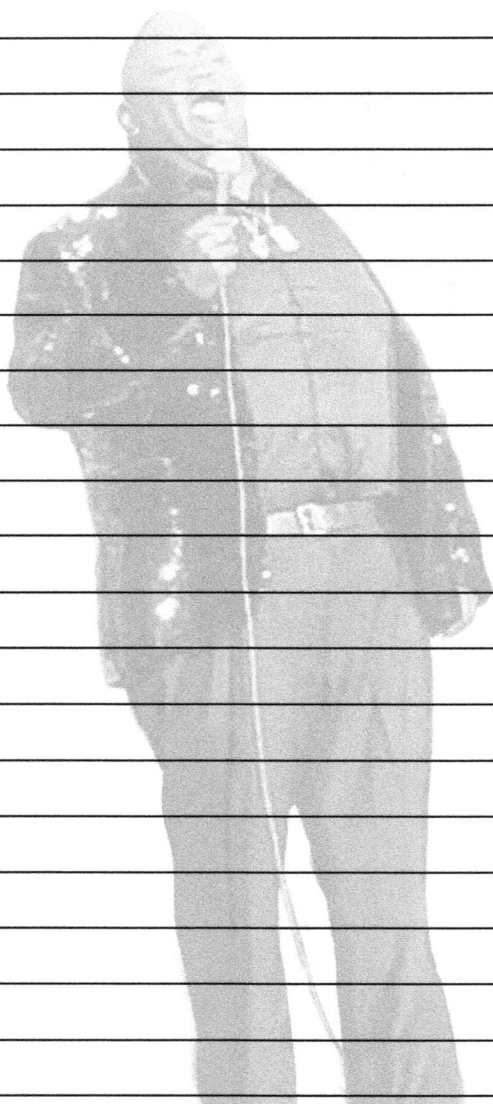

# CHAPTER 7:

# GET YOUR ASS ON STAGE

When you caught that comedy bug, it's likely that you were been a student watching comedy videos, going to live comedy nights, watching other aspiring comics and veteran comics pass or fail on the stage, and you remained steadfast on your dream to be the next comedy star.

My first chance to get on stage wasn't overnight. I had to call the comedy club every week (St. Louis Funny Bone) and put my name on the list, and I had to call back around show time to see if I made the weekly lineup. It took a month and a half or two months to make it on the open mic list. After diligently calling, my tenacity finally paid off, but when the opportunity came knocking, I went into a panic. *What the heck am I going to talk about?* This brought me to the conclusion that these techniques would be helpful:

- **Be prepared**: "How do I do this?" you may ask. There are many ways. I used to envision myself on stage telling a story.

- **Write an outline:** Another way is to write an outline of the subject you're going to talk about.

Here's a sample outline:

- o Family
- o Funny Story
- o Something relatable, like "the president sucks," the temperature, gas prices, and whatever it is you remember. You are just trying to get your feet wet and maybe do stock jokes out of a book. Don't borrow a joke from your favorite comedians. That's stealing, which is a form of plagiarism, and that's a major comedy mistake because most comedians and comediennes take pride in their work, and most of the time, they consider that as their masterpiece, their child, and no one steals a mediocre joke. They want the best one. So, basically, be original, organic, and fresh. Something you know or have experienced. The amazing thing about a joke is that it can be about the same topic, but a million people could view it differently.

A joke can be likened to an eyewitness report. You may all have seen the same situation, but everyone tells a different version some more factual, some more elaborate and/or exaggerated, but in the end, it's their point of view or story.

A stock joke is a joke that has been written by a humorist and told around the water cooler at work by a friend. However, stock jokes are only good for one thing: to teach you how to tell a joke, and it teaches you timing too. But right now, you just want to have something to talk about while you are on stage.

o Diligently look for open mic nights in your city. Not exclusively in your city but also cities near you.

o Always video-record your sets. That is one of the most effective tools I used in honing my gift because, with this tool, you can see what works and what doesn't work. You can find out why it worked or why it didn't work by your facial expression, and you can review your delivery style.

o Don't get discouraged because, the first time, you might suck ass or could be freeing.

o Develop a love for the stage and stand-up. Treat the stage like a bully trying to take your bike or your lunch, and no matter how many times he or she kicks your ass, you come back harder and harder until they get tired and leave you alone because you are kicking their ass.

o Never turn down the chance to do stage time because every stage is different, every crowd is different, and every moment is a new moment.

My first time on stage was pretty decent. I went on stage, and I winged it. I talked about things I knew about, like Mom trying to exercise at the house, and I thought it was an earthquake. I talked about being a fat man in a slim man's world, and it worked. I knew at that moment that this was the path God had directed me to, and from there, I became hungry for the stage. I lived at the comedy clubs when I wasn't working. I would watch people who were big stars then. So, I love this crazy world of stand-up. Come get your ass on stage and get addicted.

o   Also record or video the majority of your set, even if you don't have the equipment there. A fellow comic that has it or even the comedy club can do it for you—they will record your set for a nominal fee unless you're performing at Bob's Chicken Shack.

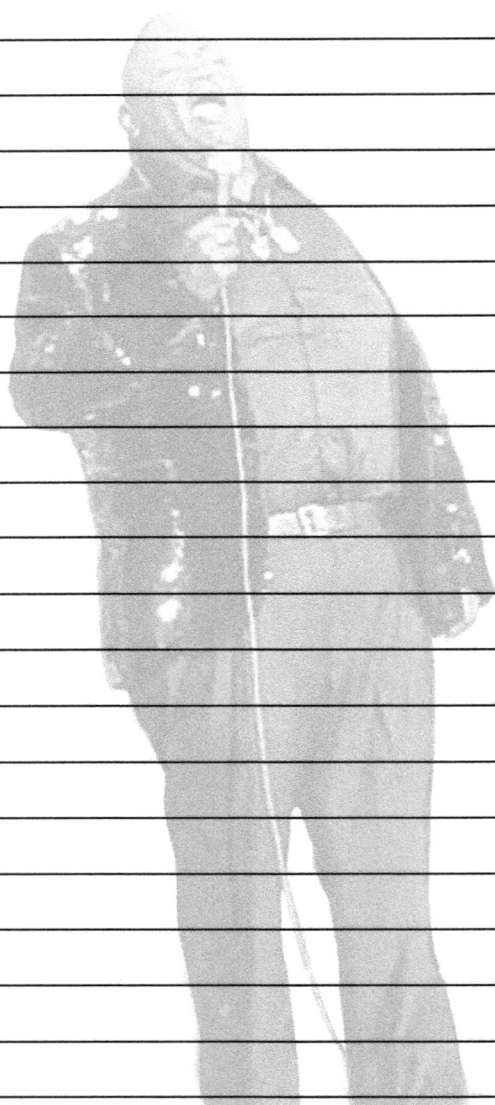

# LAVELL CRAWFORD

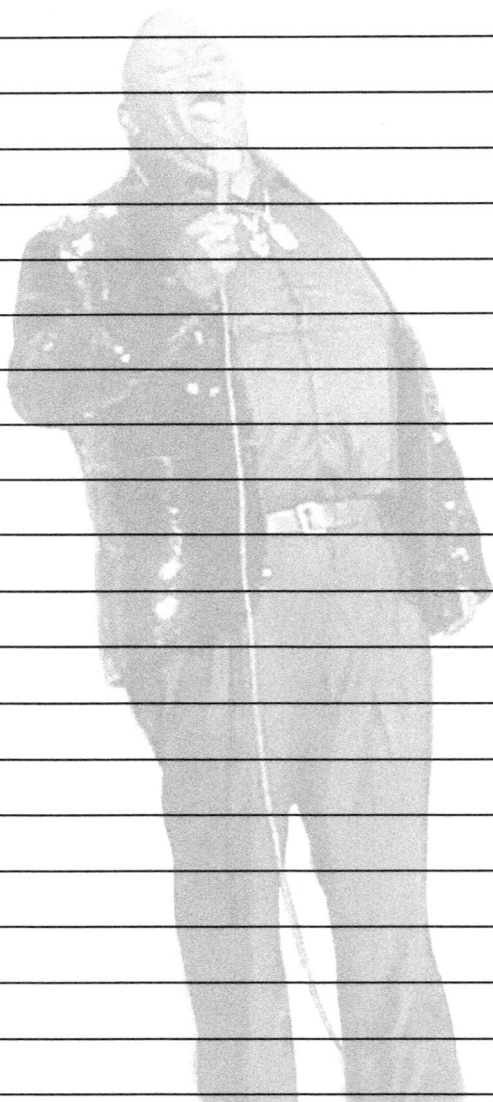

_____

_____

_____

_____

_____

_____

_____

_____

_____

_____

_____

_____

_____

_____

_____

_____

_____

_____

_____

_____

_____

_____

_____

# CHAPTER 8:

# ELEMENTS OF COMEDY

You don't have to use these elements in numerical order. As I stated, it's just a guide I used when I gained more experience on stage.

When I started, my whole mission was to get on stage, feel the audience, and to be funny enough to get the crowd's response, no matter how large or small it was. I was only hanging out with comics that had the same outlook as me. I could be a snob sometimes, honestly speaking. I don't like to be around a comic that always has to be 'on,' i.e., always trying to be funny, trying to top everyone else's joke like that puppy at the pet store hoping to get adopted or a foster child at the children's home who is almost 20 and is still looking for a home or that cerebral/political comic that thinks he or she is doing something innovative. I like being around people such that the joke flows naturally in general conversation; even if they're bouncing material off, it doesn't seem forced. In all, the main element that I really practiced was the material. That's something I strive on making my strength, and everyone has their own particular way of writing a material. Some write it out in a notebook on Post-it or iPads and even take it on stage with them. None of that felt comfortable to me. My comfort zone was and is: getting to just talk about offstage things, and then getting on stage and talking about it to strangers, and people would ask, "How do you remember what you said from show to show? Heck!" I would always respond, "I know what I said while I was up there," but then, other times, I record my act video or audio just to see where I can 'milk' that joke.

Milk is a term used in the comedy game, which is like what a farmer does to get milk out of a cow's teat squeeze as much fun out of the joke or premise. I wrote some of my favorite materials onstage, but that takes a good work ethic and love for the craft, and it will be muscle memory.

All these other elements will fall into place like puzzle pieces. So, get your ass on stage and stop asking me for advice. Get the experience for yourself.

Stay tuned to my announcements to know when I would be bringing my Q&A seminar to a comedy club in your city or near your city.

Till then, always remember the following:

- Material
- Timing
- Delivery
- Stage presence

- Stage management
- Putting up that fourth wall
- Commanding the show
- POV
- Finding your character
- Finding your voice
- Becoming fearless

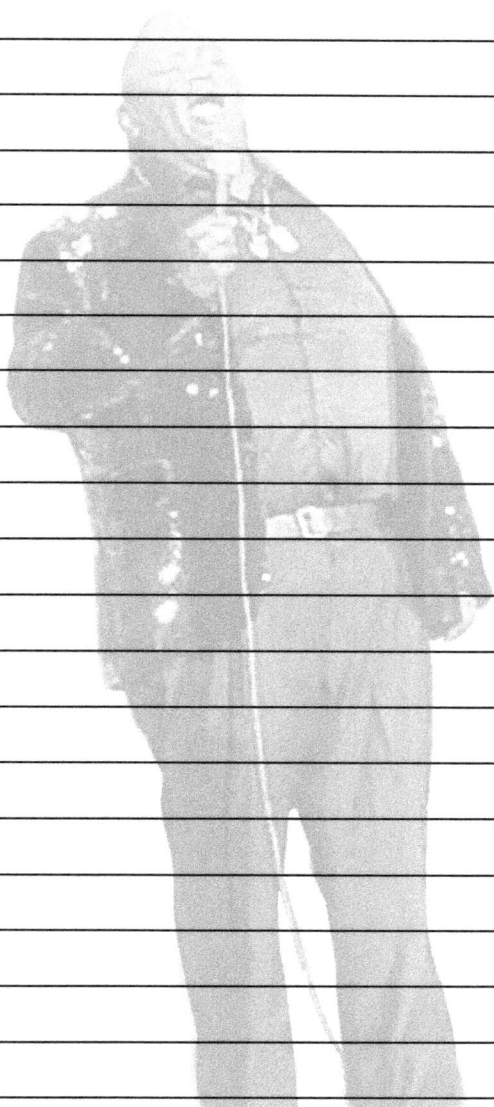

_____

_____

_____

_____

_____

_____

_____

_____

_____

_____

_____

_____

_____

_____

_____

_____

_____

_____

_____

_____

_____

_____

# LAVELL CRAWFORD

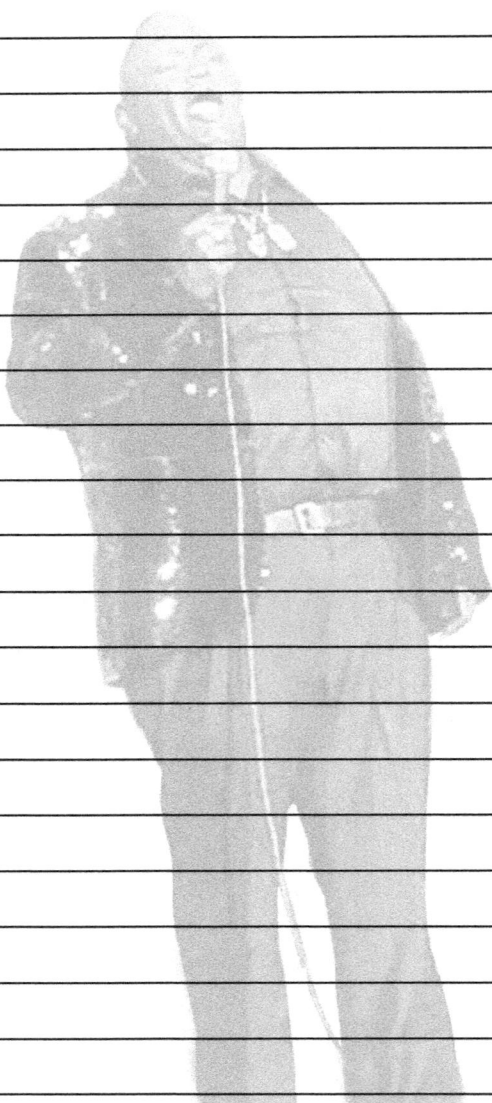

# COMEDY SCHOOL GUIDE TO STAND UP!

_____

_____

_____

_____

_____

_____

_____

_____

_____

_____

_____

_____

_____

_____

_____

_____

_____

_____

_____

_____

_____

_____

_____

# LAVELL CRAWFORD

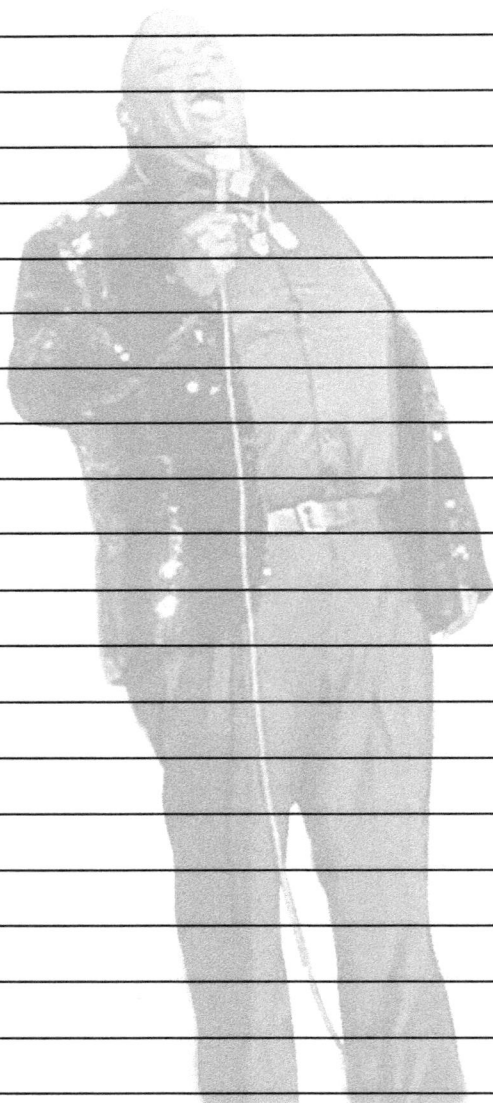

_____

_____

_____

_____

_____

_____

_____

_____

_____

_____

_____

_____

_____

_____

_____

_____

_____

_____

_____

_____

_____

_____

# COMEDY SCHOOL GUIDE TO STAND UP!

_____

_____

_____

_____

_____

_____

_____

_____

_____

_____

_____

_____

_____

_____

_____

_____

_____

_____

_____

_____

_____

_____

# ABOUT THE AUTHOR

Comedian Lavell Crawford is quickly climbing the comedic ranks and becoming one of the hottest stars in the biz today. He filmed a new one-hour special "Can A Brother Get Some Love?" in his home town of St. Louis, and it's on DVD from Entertainment One. In addition, he filmed an episode of "Workaholics" for Comedy Central, and he's been casted in a recurring role on the AMC's Emmy Award-winning "Breaking Bad." If that's not enough, he was also seen as a regular panelist on E! Entertainment's "Chelsea Lately" and a regular on "Lopez Tonight," performing in various comedy sketches on the show. From his numerous television appearances and as one of the hottest touring acts in the country, audiences are becoming increasingly familiar with Lavell's giant-sized talent.

Lavell gained huge national exposure on NBC's hit reality series "Last Comic Standing." Not only did NBC take notice, promptly signing Lavell to a holding deal with the network, but also Comedy Central, offering him his own half-hour standup special, "Comedy Central Presents: Lavell Crawford." Lavell's stand-out work includes appearances on "Shaquille O'Neal Presents: All Star Comedy Jam" which premiered on Showtime in December, "Russell Simmons' Def Comedy

Jam" on HBO, "Showtime at the Apollo," "Martin Lawrence Presents 1st Amendment," "Comic's Unleashed with Byron Allen," "Steve Harvey's Big Time," "Comedy Central's Premium Blend," "Motown Live," and "BET's Comic View." In addition, Lavell has appeared in the films "Baby's Mama Drama," "Beverlyhood," "Ghetto South Problems," and on the televised series "The Jamie Foxx Show." On stage, he played Ben in the hit play "Men Cry in the Dark" based on the Michael Baisden best seller. Lavell also recently appeared on stage with the critically acclaimed production "Friends and Lovers," a stage production based on the novel by author Eric Jerome Dickey, where he played the scene-stealing Bobby. The play also featured notable actors such as Miguel Nunez ("Juwana Man"), Leon ("The Five Heartbeats"), Monica Calhoun ("The Best Man"), Mel Jackson ("Soul Food"), and Maia Campbell ("In the House").

Endeared by audiences far and wide, Lavell has built a very strong fan base playing theatres, comedy clubs, and colleges across the nation in addition to festivals, including HBO's US Comedy Arts Festival, The Comedy Festival, and LAFFAPALOOZA—America's longest-running annual urban comedy festival.

Feel free to stay connected with Lavell Crawford by following him on:

www.Instagram.com/LavellCrawford and
www.comedianlavellcrawford.com